Travellers' Tales

ROSS & CROMARTY

GHOSTS WITCHES FOLKLORE LEGENDS STRANGE MYSTERIES AND SECRETS

Lang**Syne**
PUBLISHING
WRITING *to* REMEMBER

PUBLISHER'S NOTE

Stories in Part One were gathered orally by R Mac Donald Robertson during extensive throughout Ross and Cromarty. Many had been told round the peat fire on dark winteer nights and at ceilidhs before beeing written down and edited by journalist Jeremy Brucewatt. The stories reproduced here were first published by Oliver and Boyd in "Selected Highland Folk Tales" and "More Highland Folk Tales" and are reproduced here by arrangement with their successors Longman UK. The stories in Part Two, told in a delightful fairy tale style, were written by Helen Drever, illustrated by Mildred R Lamb, and first published by the Moray Press in "lure of the kelpie".Reproduced by permission of the copyright holders.

"Travellers'Tales:Ross and Cromarty" was published by Langsyne Publishers Ltd, Strathclyde Business Centre,120 Carstairs Street,Glasgow,G40 4JD,Tel:0141 554 9944,Fax:0141 554 9955,Email:info@scottish-memories. co.uk, www.scottish-memories.co.uk,
Printed by Digisource(GB)Livingston, Scotland.Original illustration by John Mackay in Part One are published for the first time.
I.S.B.N. 185217 199 5
Copyright Lang Syne Publishers Ltd 2005
Reprinted 2005

Introduction

Why was a fisherman sentenced to hang after being tricked by three witches? What happened to the lady who sold her soul to the Devil? Where did ghostly and ghastly visitors bring terror to a holiday home? Who haunted a castle until his walled up remains were given a proper burial? When were ghostly cries of despair heard on Loch Maree? How did a young girl break an evil spell and end up very rich indeed?

These are just some of the questions answered in this fascinating collection of folk tales and supernatural lore from Ross and Cromarty.

You can also find out about; the witch's spell that scared all the herring out of Loch Broom, the secrets of the Findhorn River, including the magic candles that offer admittance to fairy dwellings, the young men sentenced to hang seven by seven, the Prince and Princess trapped in the bodies of a horse and cat, the lights that forewarned of death, the strange sea creatures who terrified fishermen, and the Devil Piper.

Also, talking of the Devil, we discover how whisky was his very own potion, hear of a minister who exorcised a haunted dressing table, and learn of the place where no living creature would go because a mermaid murdered a human there. We also visit the island of the damned, as well as unlocking other fascinating tales and secrets from the same area's stirring past.

Happy reading!

PART ONE

The three witches of Kintail

A story of Loch Duich,
as told by Ruraidh Mor, of Ullapool

Long ago, in the village of Kintail on the shores of Loch Duich, there lived a ship's carpenter called Willie.

Now Willie's own dinghy needed mending, but neither in his workshop, nor in the village, could he find the right piece of wood. So Willie started off to the woods.

For many hours the carpenter wandered and searched among the pine trees. How long he walked before he realised that he was lost, Willie did not know, but daylight was fading and the woods were wrapped in the damp greyness of the mist.

On and on he went, always, as he thought, in the direction of Kintail. At nearly every step the track became more hazardous and the visibility became worse than ever, until, suddenly, he saw a faint glimmer of light winking thorugh the fog. When he got closer, he found that the light was emanating from a cottage window.

Groping his way to the door, Willie knocked loudly.

From inside there came the sound of shuffling feet. Slowly the door opened to reveal an old woman; she did not speak, so Willie explained his plight, and only then did she bid him enter.

Now Willie, who had been born and bred in the district and had lived all his life in Kintail, thought it rather strange that he neither recognised the aged lady nor remembered ever having seen the cottage before, and it was with a feeling of wonderment that he followed her into the kitchen, thanking her for her Highland hospitality.

Imagine his surprise when he found that there were two even older ladies seated one at each side of the peat fire. He had never seen them before either.

The first told Willie briefly that the other two were her sisters and, after introducing him, invited the now bewildered carpenter to dine with them, and, since he was very hungry, he accepted gladly and willingly took a dram.

Feeling rather better after the meal, Willie decided to agree to the sisters' suggestion that he should spend the night with them since the mist, which lingered thickly outside, was still pressing against the cottage window.

He was shown to his room — a small one, which contained among other articles of furniture, a bed, a table and chair and a large old-fashioned wooden box opposite the fireplace. The atmosphere of the place felt queer and even sinister. He began to wish that he had never entered this cottage and, for a moment, thought of leaving at once; but he was so tired that he lay down and soon fell asleep.

Willie slept soundly and did not hear the door open, nor did he hear the shuffle of the first sister's slippers as she crossed the room.

He woke with a start only with the creaking of hinges long rusty, and saw her lit by the glow from the smouldering peat fire. She was bending over the old wooden trunk at the foot of his bed, and she looked like a witch. Willie stayed very still and watched ....

The old hag searched for a while in the wooden box and then stood up — in her hand she held a small red cap. Carefully she placed it on her head and slowly she uttered the strangest words: "Here's off to London," she said.

The next moment she had disappeared up *"am farleus"* (the chimney) and Willie lay gasping with surprise and fright.

Hardly had he begun to recover a little when in shuffled the second sister and, going over to the trunk, she too took out a small red bonnet, which she placed on her head, and she, too, lifted her right arm and muttered the same words: "Here's off to London," and immediately vanished after her sister ....

Not more than a minute later, to his amazement, entered

"Here's off to London," she said

the third sister and she, too, took out a small red cap, and in like manner was spirited away up the chimney ....

Willie lay in a state of nervous bewilderment for a while, and wondered what on earth to do.

He pinched himself hard to see if he really was awake and not dreaming these strange happenings. Then he decided the best thing to do would be to get out of bed and search the house. So he crept very quietly out of the bedroom and into the kitchen; but there was no one about and he found on closer investigation that he was entirely alone in the cottage.

Willie returned to the bedroom and decided to have a look inside the trunk. There was nothing inside it but one small red cap. He lifted it out rather carefully and examined it; but it appeared to be a perfectly ordinary bonnet, so he placed it on his head.

And then Willie did a very stupid thing. He was suddenly possessed by a strong feeling of curiosity and, rather timidly, let it be said, he, too, raised his right hand and uttered the words: "Here's off to London!"

No sooner had he done so than, to his amazement, he immediately found himself walking down Bow Street in London City.

This was the London of Samuel Pepys; the London of coffee and ale houses and cobble stones, and it was into an ale house that Willie turned, and it was strange that he felt no alarm at finding himself in town when all his life had been spent in far-away Scotland; but in he went and imagine his amazement at finding the three old sisters sitting round a table drinking whisky.

They invited him over to join them for a refreshment without showing the slightest surprise.

After the four visitors had consumed their drinks, they sat for a little while watching the men of fashion who drifted in. It seemed to Willie rather strange that they were not astonished to see three such ancient witches sitting in their ale house; but no one appeared to notice anything odd about the Highlanders.

It seemed to Willie rather strange ....
no one appeared to notice anything odd ....

After standing each other a few more drams, the first sister put on the little red cap, which she had taken off on arriving in London, and this time it was her left arm which she raised before she mumbled: "Here's off back to Kintail," and vanished through the smoke-blackened oak beams.

Then the second sister put on her red bonnet and vanished after the first. Then the third sister followed her partners, leaving Willie alone at the table.

He sat there thinking of the mystery of it all, and had also just decided to return to Kintail when a waiter came up to him and presented him with the bill for the drinks.

Of course Willie had no money, so the waiter called in the manager, who sent for the police, and when Willie told them his story, they arrested him at once on a charge of witchcraft.

So poor Willie was flung into prison and eventually he was tried and found guilty — having no feasible defence to offer, and since the penalty for his crime at that time in England was death by hanging, he was sentenced to that fate.

On the day of his execution, the miserable carpenter was removed from his London prison to Hampstead. He was forced on the the scaffold and the rope was fastened about his neck.

"Have you anything to confess?" they asked.

But Willie answered, "No."

"Is there anything you wish to do or say before you meet your doom?" he was asked.

But Willie shook his head; then all of a sudden he had a great idea.

"Yes," said Willie. "I have one small request to make, and it is this; before you hang me, might I put on this small red cap I have in my pocket?"

He was told that there was no reason why he should not, so he carefully put on the red bonnet.

The huge crowd which had gathered to watch his execution saw him raise his left arm and they heard him shout out, "Here's off back to Kintail!" And before their unbelieving gaze he vanished from their sight.

And Willie? Well, he found himself back in his own workshop on the shores of Loch Duich, not only with the rope still round his neck, but with the whole gallows plank as well!.

And so there he was back in Kintail with the very piece of wood for which he had been looking for the stem of his boat when he started off on his amazing adventure. It was just exactly what he required to make his boat seaworthy and the rope made a good anchor cord ....

In some strange way Wilie had great luck in his reconstructed vessel, for he caught more fish on the first occasion he set sail on the loch than had ever been caught before in one day, and to this day the "Miracle of the Fishes" still remains the unsolved mystery of Kintail.

Willie returned to the woods to search for the cottage, but he never found it or its weird inhabitants — they had completely disappeared. All that remained was his good luck.

So he who wishes to make a good catch of fish on Loch Duich will wear a red cap or have a red "toury" on his Highland bonnet. And you who have heard the legend of Willie the carpenter and the three witches of Kintail know why.

" 'Sann aig ceann an latha a dh'innsear an sgeul."

(The fisherman narrates his tale at the end of his day's fishing.)

Lure of the Pipes

As told to me by a native of the district

The scene was the heart of Diebidale deer forest in Ross-shire, the time was nearing midnight in the late December long ago, when the "Wee People" danced on the top of the bogs that even a wild duck could not cross without breaking the surface. Halfway up one of the hills, known as Corrie Glas, stood Big John Clach-na-Harnich, and beside him were his two famous black dogs — a dog and a bitch. Big John was the head stalker on Diebidale, and he had been out all day and most of the night after the hinds, which they were shooting off. It had turned out to be a wild night, with a half moon; and John had taken shelter for a while against the buffetings of the storm.

At last the night cleared a bit and he started for home. As it was late, he decided to go round the side of the hill and take a short cut home. He had been that road often before, and knew every step of it, and he could also jump the Poacher's Pool at Allt a'choin (The Dog's Burn) and still cut a few more miles off his road.

If there was one thing on earth Big John loved besides good whisky, it was the pipes, and as he came near Allt a'choin, he thought he heard bagpipe music. He stopped and listened, and sure enough, there it was, away to his right; and that piper could play! He was playing "Braham Castle," and John never heard it played so well before. He could not resist the music and started to walk towards it. He wondered as he went along who the piper could be, and what possessed him to come there and play on a night like that. As he neared the place where the sounds came from, the moon went behind the clouds and it became very dark.

Things seemed to become very still as he walked on, and

the sound of the pipes grew louder. The piper was now playing a reel — the finest reel John ever heard; and through the music he thought he heard hooching. All of a sudden, he saw a light, and going nearer, he saw a fail-roofed house. John knew he was not very far by now from the Poacher's Pool and Rory-the-Glen's "Black bothy"; but he could not remember ever seeing this place before. The sound of the pipes drew him on however, and he went forward to the door. But here a queer thing happened — the black bitch which would tackle the biggest stag in Diebidale, would not go another step. John stopped, and tried to coax her on, but she would not move, and lay down. Then John remembered that a bitch would not follow her master if the Unknown was in front. He was shaken at this; but the lure of the pipes was too great, and he said, "Very well, you can stay here; as long as I have Black Simon with me and Killsure (his gun) under my arm, I'll face anything."

The piper was now playing "Tulloch Gorm," and what a piper — the time he kept! Just as John went up to the door, it opened, and an old woman said — "Come in John, I'm sure you will be near starved to death with the cold." John thanked her, and said he would come in for a minute or two and hear the pipes. As he entered the house he took off his bonnet, and the old woman made to take it from him; but Black Simon, snarling and growling, snatched the bonnet out of his hand and held it in his mouth. The old woman then opened the kitchen door; and the sight that met John, he'll never forget. The house was full of men and girls. They were the finest looking girls he had ever seen. They were nearly all dressed the same, in long frocks of a queer bluish-red colour; the men had greenish-red clothes. John had ears only for the piper however; and he looked round to see where he was.

There he stood, near to the bed-closet door, and behind the spinning wheel to give room to the dancers. John was stunned when he saw the piper. Of all the pipers he had ever seen or heard about, this one was the King. He had on the full Highland dress; but for the life of him John could not tell the tartan. And the pipes! what pipes! — solid gold mounted —and as he played the Reel-o'-Tulloch, John thought he could see the blue sparks flying from his fingers and smoke coming from the chanter.

The music stopped, and the piper looked at John and smiled; but never spoke.

The only one that spoke of the whole company was the old woman, who then asked John if he would take a dram. He said he would, and she gave him a glass of good stuff. If the music was good, the whisky was better. As soon as he took the first sip, he thought his whole body was on fire right to the soles of his feet.

John drained the glass, and then the piper started to play again — a schottishe this time — and the best-looking of the girls came towards John holding out her hands, smiling at him and silently inviting him to dance. The whisky had done its work well; and John thought he could manage the dance fine, and was on the point of taking the girl in his arms, when Black Simon again jumped in front of him. John looked down at the dog, wondering what was wrong with him, and then he saw, peeping from below the girl's long frock, instead of dainty feet, two horses' hooves. He drew back frightened out of his wits; and then looking towards the closet door where the piper stood, he saw a long red streak coming oozing out from below the door. He knew then the company he was in, and also that his end was near, and shouted "God help me!" He could not have chosen better words, for all at once he saw the faces change, the piper's tartan turned to red, and over the blow-stock of the pipes, from which smoke and sparks emanated, he saw the face of Lucifer himself grinning at him.

He took his only chance, and with one bound, reached the door and turned to call Black Simon, who had twice that night saved him, and was doing it for a third time — for as John sprang for the door, the dog sprang at Nick; and as John turned, he saw Old Horny draw the dirk from its sheath (still wet with the blood of its last victim) and raise it to kill Black

*John, fast as he was, found he was no match
for the one who followed*

Simon.

Quick as a flash, John's up with "Killsure" and let drive with both barrels; but that was all the good it did, for John, who was hardly ever known to miss, saw the lead splash on the wall behind, after going harmlessly through Old Nick.

John then bolted, and ran as hard as he could for the Poacher's Pool; but fast as he was, he found he was no match for the one who followed. Looking back, he saw the Monster, and on each side of him two of the girls, now howling fiends, with flames of fire streaming from their heads in place of the fair hair they had earlier. He could hear the clatter of their horses' hooves as they raced over the rocks and heather.

John heard the gurgle of the water in the Poacher's Pool, and made a last supreme effort to reach it. Better to die in the cool water among the salmon, he thought, than be torn to bits by fingers of fire.

Then just as Old Nick raised his bloody dirk to strike, across the water at Rory-the-Glen's a cock crew in the morning. John fell unconscious on the brink of the Pool, and it was hours after when he came to, to find his two dogs licking his face. "Oh," said he, "Black Simon, I thought that your end came as the dirk fell"; but then Black Simon rolled over on his back, and John saw on the dog's breast four white hairs, and he knew that the Devil was powerless against the black dog as long as he had those hairs.

And so to this day, if you listen at Poacher's Pool, you will hear in the running water the sound of the pipes, on nights when the "Wee People" dance on the bogs, and the wind blows round Corrie Glas.

Phantom of Skibo

Before Andrew Carnegie bought Skibo Castle, it is said its corridors often echoed to unearthly screams and the apparition of a terrified woman would go flitting through the house. The story goes that earlier last century the castle was left in charge of a manservant, who induced a local girl to visit him there. One night she did not return home, and it was widely believed that she had been murdered, although nothing was found to incriminate the man. Shortly after he left and went abroad the hauntings began, and went on for many years, until while repairs were being carried out the bones of a woman were found embedded in the wall. The remains were buried in the local churchyard, and thereafter it is said the haunting ceased.

The woman in the mirror

Strange and fearful things were said to be happening in and around an old house on the outskirts of Ardgay.

A woman said that one night the kettle was lifted right off the peat fire by unseen hands in front of her eyes, and that she heard the pots and pans jumping about in the scullery.

So bad did these hauntings become, that she called upon the minister for protection. When he arrived in his dog-cart, a shower of loose stones descended as if from nowhere. This was followed by a battery of turnips and potatoes from the adjoining farmyard, but his reverence escaped being hit.

Bible in hand, the minister said in Gaelic:— "Whatever happens, I must exorcise this spirit," and being a courageous man, he volunteered to sleep in the haunted house.

He saw reflected in the mirror a black figure

When the door mysteriously burst open about midnight, he suddenly remembered he had left his Bible downstairs; so he went and brought it up and locked the door again.

Approaching the dressing-table, he saw reflected in the mirror the large black figure of a woman standing behind him in the room. When he turned round he was quite alone, although he could distinctly hear footsteps approaching nearer and nearer to where he stood in the candle-light.

He laid the Bible on the dressing-table and offered up a prayer, asking the unquiet spirit to go for good. Immediately it did so, and there was no more trouble.

Afterwards it was discovered that a maid-servant had suffocated her male child in a drawer in the dressing-chest, over eighty years before, in the very same room.

Isle of the damned

She lured his frail boat to the treacherous rocks

There are many parts of the Scottish Highlands where mysteries are still unsolved. In certain districts of Wester Ross a belief in the supernatural still prevails. "It is the land of the edge of moorlands and the ruins of forests and the twilight before dawn, and strange knowledge dwells in it." The depths and remoteness of the solitude, the huge peaks, the deep chasms between the rocks, the dark gloom of the primeval forests, the deep black lochs — are full of associations of awe and grandeur and mystery.

In the dark waters of Loch Torridon, there is a tiny weather-beaten rocky islet of not more than two acres, adorned with fir trees and grasses. It is locally known as *Eilean-nan-Sithean* (Fairy Island).

No one, it is said, has set foot on its shores for years. The Fairy Isle does not like to be visited, and the inhabitants of Shieldaig, the nearest hamlet, avoid the place. They do not use its rich grass for grazing their cattle and sheep, for it is said to be haunted by an evil spirit. At night-time, when the wind moans in the corries, they whisper, round the peat fire, the legend of a fisherman who wooed a mermaid and later deserted her. She, in turn, lured his frail boat to the treacherous rocks of *Eilean-nan-Sithean,* and dragged him to his doom in the loch.

Ever since that day, no living creature has lived for more than a few hours on it, and no birds ever rest or nest there.

"The Lights" on Loch Kinellan

A considerable time ago, a number of school children were spending their Christmas holidays at Strathpeffer. They went down one morning to call on an old woman who had a small croft. There had been a hard frost for the past week and the whole country-side was ice-bound.

The boys told the old woman of their intention to go sliding and skating on the frozen waters of Loch Kinellan on the following day. She raised her hands in protest, and in commanding tones, said: "Last night, I saw the lights on the

The ice gave way with a noise
that echoed amongst the hills

loch, which from the time of my parents downwards, are a sure sign of disaster. On no account venture on to the ice, for each time I see the lights on the loch, they foretell a drowning in the parish."

The boys took the old woman's warning. The following night there was a rapid thaw. The ice gave way with a noise which echoed amongst the hills, and three local children, who had been sliding on the frozen loch, fell through and were drowned.

The Black Rock of Novar

The Allt Graat — "ugly burn" — flows out of Loch Glass at the northern base of Ben Wyvis, and along its whole course seaward displays an unbelievable succession of cliffs and waterfalls. The stream, a short distance from the village, on the estate of Novar, backed by the fine mountain of Fyrish, rushes down a glacier rut, composed of sandstone strata for nearly two miles in length of an average of over one hundred feet in depth. This remarkable gorge is said to be fully five times deeper than it is broad. The gully is in many places overgrown and hidden by thick foliage; while along the rocky channel below, a roaring torrent is heard rumbling with violence, though invisible from the banks above. This particular stretch of the stream is locally known as "The Black Rock of Novar."

"The precipices are green with some moss or byssus, that, like the miner, chooses a subterranean habitat — for here the rays of the sun never fall; the trees, fast anchored in the rock, shoot out their branches across the opening, to form a thick tangled roof at the height of 150 ft overhead — while from the recesses within, where the eyes fail to penetrate, there issues a combination of the strangest and wildest sounds ever yet produced by water — there is the deafening rush of the torrent blent as with the clang of hammers, the roar of vast bellows, and the confused gabble of 1000 voices .... Now we hear a sulky roar, as of a wild beast crawling from his den; again a weary sigh, as of a hapless, hopeless lover."

At times it sounds an eerie wail, as of an infant crying in the night; at times a wild dirge, sinking and swelling, as when the clan bewails its fallen chief. Many animals have met their doom by falling into this abyss, as the top of it is not fenced off. On one occasion, I am told that a dog in pursuit of a roe deer fell headlong into the chasm; but emerged unscathed several hundred yards downstream at Pol Slugain near the entrance to the Black Rock, wagging its tail. On another occasion it is said that a sailor fell off the old wooden bridge — which at one time spanned the head of the ravine — the only man known to survive the terrible ordeal. According to the story, he held on to the branch of a tree until rescued by a rope lowered to him from the bank above.

A short distance from the entrance to the Black Rock, there is a cave by the water's edge, only approachable by rope from above. This cavern is situated in the rock at the base of a perpendicular waterfall of some 80 feet in height. The cave in olden days was used for making whisky, and the fumes from the still were cleverly concealed in the spray of the descending water.

Many years ago a young Englishman of noble birth on holiday in Ross-shire went one night to a Highland Ball at Alness. For some time he sat alone, looking on at the dances which alas were foreign to him, when suddenly he noticed a beautiful young lady — lovely as a fairy-tale princess, with hair black as night and eyes like dark pools. He asked her to dance, and they took to the floor to the lilting strains of a waltz. She was as light as thistle down in his arms, and her slender feet scarcely seemed to touch the floor. The soft sweet music and the beauty of his partner acted on the young man like a potent drug. The music ceased, and they wandered arm in arm off the floor. Then he saw a servant approaching to drive the lady home.

"Before you go, will you tell me who you are?" he asked. Smiling sadly she shook her head, and with a sigh replied: "Alas, I cannot." Soon the carriage and its fair occupant had disappeared from sight, and his curiosity piqued, the young man began to question the other dancers about the identity of the lovely lady who looked so sad.

"She is the Lady of Balconie," he was told. On pressing for further information, he learned that there was a strange mystery about her. She loved to walk alone at night along the banks of the Allt Graat, by the Black Rock of Novar, and the fear-haunted surroundings of this dark chasm seemed to possess for her an uncanny fascination.

Discarding all warnings to shun the spot, he resolved to visit it the next night. His mission was not in vain. He reached the Black Rock as evening was drawing to a close. The surroundings were awesome enough to strike terror into the boldest heart. Here they met, high above the chasm, and embraced among the swirling wreaths of mist that eddied unceasingly over the edge of the precipice; while around them the night-wind shrieked and moaned like a soul in torment, and far below the waters of the black cauldron seethed in fury. To the accompaniment of the roaring of the waters, the Lady of Balconie told him her sad story.

Some years before, a serious illness, while in her teens, had robbed her of her beauty, of which she was very vain. She had entered into a compact with the Devil that if he made her the most beautiful of women for the next five years, she would give herself up to him, body and soul, at the end of that time. As soon as the unholy bargain was struck, she had regretted it. She had been lovely and sought after for these five years, but now the time had come for her to fulfil her part of the bargain. It was here that the Devil would come to claim her. Even as she spoke, a tall, stately figure loomed up before them through the mist and in commanding tones called the lady to follow him.

The young man felt her slipping silently from his grasp over the dizzy brink of the gorge. As she sank from sight she threw a bunch of keys upwards to him. Her aim, however, was wide of the mark, and as the keys of Balconie fell back into the depths below, they struck a projecting boulder, on the surface of which they left a permanent indentation. They were red hot from contact with the foul fiend. With a wild cry of despair, the young Englishman dived after her into the black pool, only to be dashed to pieces on the rocks below.

Long afterwards, an angler belonging to the district, while fishing upstream, in order to lessen the load took from his basket a number of trout and hid them by the burn-side near the Black Rock. On his return, he found that the fish had mysteriously disappeared, all that remained of his catch being a trail of silvery scales along the grass by the river's edge Determined to catch the otter, which he imagined responsible for this depredation, he followed the trail, which led downwards over many a slippery ledge to a gloomy cave, the entrance to which was guarded by two large savage dogs. Inside he could see, busily engaged in baking, a beautiful maiden in a dress of a bygone age. Stories he had heard as a boy came back to his mind, and he knew that he was looking on the lovely Lady of Balconie, who, a century before, had disappeared with such tragic suddenness.

When he had recovered from his amazement, he tried to persuade her to flee with him; but with terrified glances behind her, she shook her head and motioned him imperatively away. She thereupon took hold of a mass of leaven which lay on the table, flung a piece at each of the dogs, and waved her hand to the fisherman to leave the cave. After repeated entreaties, the angler sadly bade her farewell, and retraced his steps to the top of the cliff. Nor was he ever afterwards able to find the cavern.

Local tradition attributes the disappearance of the Lady of Balconie to none other than the Prince of Darkness himself, and he it is who keeps her prisoner. When the mists swirl among the tree-tops over the ravine, the villagers say she is busy at her baking, and on moonlight nights when the river is in flood and the wind moans in the gullies, her wistful shade is to be seen at the Black Rock searching for her English lover.

> They named it Allt Graat — Ugly Burn,
> This water through the crevice hurled,
> Scouring the entrails of the world —
> Not ugly in the rising smoke
> That clothes it with a rainbowed cloak,
> But slip a foot on frost-spiked stone
> Above this rock-lipped Phlegethon

And you shall have
The Black Rock of Kiltearn
For tombstone, grave
And trumpet of your resurrection.

Big Rory

Close to Braemore Lodge, Braemore Junction, in Wester Ross, are four large stones placed, it is said, to mark the leap of Rory. The place, known as Leum Ruaraidh, commands a magnificent view of the Big Strath. The local tradition is as follows:

Rory was born in Strathnasealg, and when as a child he was sent by his parents to keep the bull from the croft, he struck the bull such a smack on the ear that the animal fell dead. Later years found Rory turning his attention to smuggling, and he carried on his business in Achindrean. Eventually he was outlawed and confined in Edinburgh Castle.

At this time there was an English champion who lived at the expense of the City of Perth till someone could be found to thrash him. The governor of the jail, hearing of Rory's strength, communicated with headquarters. Rory was interviewed, and freedom and money promised if he would beat the Englishman. The encounter took place in Holyrood Palace. Rory hit his adversary over the heart with a terrific blow, and the Englishman fell dead.

Rory was a free man and made for the Big Strath. He first caught sight of Loch Broom from a spot to the north of Braemore House. Here, he gave three terrific leaps of joy which are marked by stones. It is said that Rory also built the Tower of Fairburn.

The Destitution Road

Morag MacIntosh, of Strath, Gairloch, over 140 years ago, saw distress and famine in Wester Ross fully two years before the actual famine occurred. She had, of course, the second sight. So it happened, just as she foretold, that in 1846, great distress and poverty struck the Dundonnell district, at the head of Little Lochbroom, and the road between Dundonnell and Ullapool, to this day is known as the Destitution Road. The potato disease, shrivelling the shaws and blackening the potatoes, brought distress and destitution to a country almost entirely dependent on the potato as its main source of food for both man and beast.

Starvation stared the people in the face. A Destitution Committee was set up in Edinburgh, urged on by the Lady Mackenzie of Gairloch of the day. Grants were given and work was provided, and the Gairloch-Loch Maree road was one of the first schemes to be really effective as a measure to provide work, food and money for the starving Highlanders. A Gaelic tune recording (Rathad Ur a Ghearrloch) is still heard at the ceilidh.

Mr Hugh Mackenzie of Dundonnell made a similar application on behalf of his tenants, and after customary delay and consideration, the Destitution Committee sent Captain Webb with two privates to map and line out the road. The ultimate plans were sent from Woolwich and were sanctioned by Admiral Russell Elliot of Appleby Castle. Eventually, Mr Mackenzie received the whole grant and the plans. Work was immediately commenced on the construction of a road from Dundonnell by Fain to Braemore. This was achieved with some difficulty, on account of the difficult and dangerous contour of the land, the route lying as it does over extensive peat bogs, ravines and deep gorges; but it resulted in a well-laid track known to this day as the Destitution Road.

How the Herring came to Loch Broom

Long, long ago, immense shoals of herring regularly visited the Island of Lewis, but never Loch Broom, Loch a'Bhraoin, the Big Loch — for the witches saw to that. Accordingly, women on the lochside consulted together, and decided to terminate the witches' spell. They had a silver herring fish moulded and presented it to a strong crew of Loch Broom fishermen. The lads set sail for the Lews in a boat painted black on one side and red on the other. Having reached their destination, they refreshed themselves, and afterwards they attached the silver fish to a length of line and, trailing the lure after them, set off back for Ullapool.

In no time they were followed by vast shoals of herring which continued to follow the course between Morefield and Druimnagiuthas, where the loch gets narrower, and there the fish went beyond the boat. The vessel could not make headway with the herring on either side of her, so they pulled the silver fish on board, and the crew had to row to get ahead of the shoals of fish. They led the shoals up the loch as far as Letters, and here they flung their silver fish into Loch Broom in order to keep the fish always there. That is how the herring were enticed into the Big Loch.

The Ghost in the Copper

I heard an old man tell the following story, many years ago, round a peat fire at a ceilidh in a certain cottage on the outskirts of Strathpeffer.

"Peril by sea or land," he began, "even peril in battle, count as mere nothing when compared with the terrors of an encounter with ghosts. For my own part I can only marvel at the rare pluck and courage of my friends Mrs Wallace and Mrs Fraser during their experiences at a mansion they had rented for a holiday in central Scotland."

One day Mrs Wallace went to explore the buildings and came to a lumber room which had once been a laundry. Here she was startled to hear a strange noise made by something in the copper. Everyone knows the dimensions of a laundry copper; but when she went to peep into this one, expecting to find a rat, she found herself looking into a deep and sepulchral well, at the bottom of which was — a man.

"I could see him distinctly," she said later, "owing to a queer kind of light that seemed to emanate from every part of him. He was draped in a fantastic costume that might have been a kimono or one of those flowery dressing-gowns worn by our great-great-grandfathers.

"He was bending over a box, which he was doing his best to conceal under a pile of debris, and it was this noise that attracted me. Too intent on his work, he was apparently unaware of my close proximity until satisfied that the box was well hidden, when he straightened his back and looked up. His face frightened me; not that it was anything out of the normal, either in feature or complexion; but it was that expression — the look of evil joy that suffused every lineament before he saw me, changing to one of the most diabolical fury as our eyes met. I was at first too transfixed to do more than stare, and it was only when crouching down, he took a sudden and deliberate spring at the wall, and began to climb it like a spider that I regained possession of my limbs and fled for my life."

There can be no doubt that Mrs Wallace did quite a proper thing in bolting. When men begin to climb laundry coppers after the fashion of spiders, there must always be an element of danger in encountering them. Of course when Mrs Wallace told her mother what had happened she was laughed at, but one night matters came to a terrible climax; her bedroom became haunted. Petrified with fear, unable to move, she could only listen as whatever it was crossed towards her bed.

"It was an enormous black cat — a demon cat stalking over my legs, its tail almost perpendicular, and swaying slightly like the nodding plumes of a hearse, it squatted down between the bed-posts opposite, transfixing me with a stare full of malevolent meaning."

A cat's tail swaying like the plumes of a hearse must indeed have been a terrible sight. One would readily forgive the lady if at this stage she even buried her head in the bedclothes. But fortunately for the members of the Society for Phsychical Research she did nothing of the kind. The place was a veritable chamber of horrors, for away in the corner of the chimney she saw the spider-climbing man — nursing a baby! Again I will quote her own words.

"I glanced from him to the cat, and from the cat back again to him. Of my two enemies which was most to be feared? . . . . Mine was indeed a most unenviable position, and I was despairing of its ever being otherwise when a sudden transmutation in the man sent a flow of icy blood to my heart. He no longer regarded his burden indifferently — he scowled at it. The scowl deepened, the utmost fury pervaded his features, converting them into those of a demon. He got up, gnashed his teeth, stamped on the ground and lifting up the child dropped it head first into the fire. I saw it fall, I heard it burn. I shrieked. The effect was electric. Dropping the poker with which he had been holding down the baby the inhuman monster swung round and saw me. The expression on his face at once became hellish, absolutely hellish. My only chance of salvation now lay in making the greatest noise possible, and I began to shout lustily for help. At this, the man gave a signal, and the black cat sprang."

It is small wonder that the lady fainted, and when she came to herself, she found she was alone. It remains a marvel that she was able to reveal so much of the doings of these ghostly and ghastly visitors.

The Black Bothy of Wyvis

In the parish of Alness, about three-quarters of a mile north of the Black Rock of Novar, and just below Marshall's Gate, there is a very old churchyard, now overgrown by trees, among which the old-fashioned slab gravestones can still be seen. One of these gravestones was of particular interest to the famous smuggler Old Donald Fraser and his cronies; for below the stone there was a grave — empty except when a wee barrel or two reposed in it.

Between the churchyard and the Black Rock, below Assynt House, are the White Wells, where it was known the Little People came at night to drink of the glorious water and dance on the great big water-lily leaves. Old Donald in his nocturnal journeyings to and from the Black Rock and the old churchyard often saw the Little People, and it was they who taught him to make tea from the grandavy plant that grows at White Wells, and which was in great demand in the North as a cure for eczema.

Donald's Black Bothy was in the Black Rock just above Pool Luchish (Pool of the Swallows), and was so well hidden that it was never discovered by the gaugers. In fact this bothy was so safe that other smugglers in the district, although they did not actually know where the place was, used to take their whisky to the old churchyard, where Donald collected it, took it to his bothy and disposed of it as occasion arose. One of the smugglers was known as Wyvis John — a particular friend of Donald's. His bothy was on the north-west shoulder of Ben Wyvis, 2000 feet above Loch Glass, and could only be reached by a secret path known only to a select few, among them Donald. Wyvis John was one of those who used the empty grave, but when he was on one of his trips there, he was never seen on the road, but it was known he crossed Scoro-halter in the dead of night, which brave men would hardly tackle through the day.

One night before the Old New Year, Old Donald got a message that there was something in the grave, and accordingly, as was his habit, at twelve midnight he went to collect it. He moved back the gravestone, and had just pulled the barrel out of the grave when he noticed a figure standing by watching him.

Donald at once thought: "This is a gauger and I am caught." The figure, however, seemed to guess what was in Donald's mind, for it spoke and said: "Have no fear, Donald, for I am no gauger; but a man after your own heart." Donald took comfort in this and asked the stranger who he was and how he knew what was in the grave. To this the stranger replied: "It does not matter what is my name, and it is few graves that I do *not* know what is in them." Donald replied: "You'll be a minister or a doctor, then, and out for a bit of sport like myself." The stranger said: "Maybe; but what I want is, for you to take me to your bothy and let me see how you draw the whisky, for I hear you are the best in all Scotland at it."

This was true, for when a special brew was due to be taken off, Donald was often sent for by the other smugglers. This remark of the stranger's pleased Donald greatly, and he went nearer to him. He saw that he was a tall, dark man wearing a long Inverness cloak down to his heels, with a reddish tam-o-shanter on his head.

Donald said to him: "I would be very pleased, indeed, to let you see me at my work; but our worm is broken just now and won't be ready for a week yet; but if you'll meet me three nights hence at this same time at the east end of Loch Glass, I'll take you to a place where you'll be welcome, and you'll see all you want to see." To this the stranger agreed, and they parted.

Donald went on his way to the Black Rock, and when passing the White Wells he heard the Little People whispering to him: "Be careful, Donald Fraser. Be careful, Donald Fraser." Donald thought they meant his descent into the Rock with his burden, and thought no more about it. At the appointed time he was waiting at the east end of Loch Glass. He felt ill-at-ease, although he often met his friends there. The loch tonight seemed darker and more foreboding than ever. It was dead calm, and not a sound could be heard.

Donald was looking at the water, when suddenly there was a sound at his back, like the sigh of the wind in the heather, and when he turned, there was the stranger, dressed in the same way as when they had first met. Donald said: "I did not hear you coming," and the stranger smiled. Donald said: "You are late, but I thought you might have gone wrong on the road." "Oh no," said the stranger, "I had other business on hand, but now I am ready, so we'll go." Donald and he set out for their two mile walk along the lochside before they would reach the secret path. They talked as they went along, about brewing of whisky, about which the stranger seemed to know quite a lot.

When they reached the path, Wyvis John was waiting for them: he had received word that Donald was bringing a friend. John welcomed the stranger, but no name was asked, as it was thought that he was some "toff" out for a bit of sport. After a pull at the bottle which John had brought, they started the climb up the mountain. At last they reached the cave and went inside. There they met half a dozen others — shepherds and gillies from round about, and a well-known innkeeper from Garve.

Smuggling at that time was carried on in a big way. After the hospitality of the cave had been duly sampled, the main business of the night was started. The brew was ready, and Old Donald took his seat at the end of the worm and commenced to draw off the foreshot. This proceeding requires a great deal of skill coupled with strong lungs, and takes some time, but at last the job was done and the clear spirit began to drip slowly from the worm into a stone jar. Donald then sat back well pleased with his effort and, turning to the stranger, said: "How's that?"

The stranger said: "Grand, but I think I could get a bigger flow." Donald was at once on his mettle and said: "Here, have a go at it." Nothing loth, the stranger took Donald's place, put his mouth to the worm and commenced to suck; but first he asked that some more fire be put under the still.

After several long intakes of breath, the stranger drew breath, and when he did so the eyes of his audience nearly popped out of their heads, for instead of the spirit dripping from the end of the worm, it was pouring in a stream! The stranger then called for a horn, and filling it half up, he added as much cold water, and handed it to Wyvis John, saying: "Try that." John took the horn and drank it off. A look of the greatest pleasure crossed his face and he smacked his lips. He said nothing, however, but handed the horn back, at the same time pointing to the others. Again and again the horn was filled, till each one had drunk — all except the stranger. Then tongues were loosened and everybody was talking at once. Never had whisky been brewed like this.

The stranger said: "Drink up, my friends; I can get gallons more from here." Then began the greatest drinking-bout that was ever seen in the country, while the stranger looked on with a sardonic smile. Soon the talk, cleverly led by the stranger, turned to the sports, so dearly loved by the Highlander, of running and jumping and feats of strength. The stranger suggested it would be a great jump from the cave to the loch below.

"What!" said one of the younger gillies, mad with the drink. "I could jump to the other side of Loch Glass from here." "So could I," shouted one of the others, and again a third and a fourth, till the whole lot, even Old Donald, were willing to take the hellish leap. The stranger egged them on, saying, "To the one who jumps farthest, I'll give the secret of how I drew the whisky."

The gillie who first said he would make the leap then, without more ado, ran to the back of the cave to give himself a running spring from the ledge at the mouth; and was on the point of starting, when something happened.

From out of the darkness at the back of the cave came a snow-white ptarmigan, that Wyvis John had found the August before, with a broken wing, and had taken it to the cave, where it had stayed ever since. Little did he know that the bird was to be the means of saving his life and that of the others; for, as it came forward, it gave the strange compelling cry of the moor-fowl: "Go-back, go-back!" When the stranger saw the white bird in the cave, he sprang back to get away from it, and the men saw him change. The tippets of the Inverness cloak now seemed to be a pair of black, shining wings, while the face and head appeared to be that of the Devil himself!

The ptarmigan cried again; and then, with a horrible yell of baffled rage and despair, "Domhnull Dubh" hurled himself from the edge into the loch below.

The innkeeper, who was nearest to the entrance, shouted to the others: "My God, look — the loch's on fire!" Sure enough, they saw that where the stranger had entered, the loch seemed to be ablaze, and the cascading water from the splash seemed like shooting flames. It remained like that for a moment or so, then darkness fell once more. The fright sobered them, and when Wyvis John looked at his still and worm, he found but a molten mass of copper, and not a trace of the glorious whisky in the stone jar.

When the story was told afterwards, it was said that they had all got drunk, and that the fire had melted the copper, and that it was the morning sun shining on the loch they had seen; but as Donald said — whoever saw a peat fire melt copper, and whoever saw the morning sun shine on Loch Glass in the dead of winter?

And when Donald passed the White Wells again, the Little People were singing; and they even, he said, helped him to carry the little barrels. And the grandavy plant still grows at the White Wells, and there is still an empty grave below Marshall's Gate.

Strange Sea Creatures

A native of Wester Ross, whose integrity is beyond reproach, tells how on Tuesday, April 7, 1953, while a boat from Dibaig was crossing down to Gairloch to the fishing ground, the crew observed, as they supposed, a dead man, seeing only his head. They steered towards him. When about 20 yards off, however, they were surprised to see him rise out of the water to near the waist. They then had a good look at him, and he is said to have possessed an uncommonly big nose and long black hair. Then he dived headlong out of sight. The crew of the boat were frightened and returned home. The skipper of the boat said he had seen a mermaid before, and is positive this was a man.

This point, called An Rudha Lochdreine, seems to be associated with strange creatures. A man who has now gone over to the majority, while fishing with a rod, saw a big red horse passing very near the shore.

A brother of the same story-teller, who spent his days on the sea, said his ship was once moored, when they saw a man coming up on one of the chains, and that they shot him. He then fell into the water, which suddenly became red with blood. Soon they heard an unearthly roar, then another and another further away, as if there were two or three of them about the ship; but were not troubled any further by the inhabitants of the deep. It is said that the man which the Dibaig fisherman saw was of a prodigious size.

Another strange tale from Gairloch describes how a certain boat was out on the loch and a hand came up and grasped the side of the boat and dragged the side down until they cut the hand off.

Part Two

Secrets of the Findhorn River

Do you know the Findhorn River, which a famous scholar once called the loveliest river in Britain?

It rises away in the heart of the Monadh Liath Mountains, and makes its way — a cheerful, brawling young stream — for about ten miles, through a range of desolate hills whose height averages three thousand feet.

It is not an easy river to follow, but remember — you who set out to try it — that of all rivers in Scotland the Findhorn repays you best for a difficult walk; for beauty in ample variety, and old romantic story are in every mile of its course.

No sounds from the outer world penetrate the upper reaches of the river, and all you may expect to hear is Nature's own music — the grouse cock answering the call of the water ousel, the belling of some large stag which stands — fit model for a Landseer — on a point of rock several hundred feet above the river, the musical disturbance of the water as a herd of red deer swims across. If you are fortunate you may even see an eagle or a pair of eagles soaring majestically away above the mountain tops.

Wolves lingered in the recesses of the Monadh Liath Mountains longer than in any other part of Scotland, and the last one was killed by MacQueen of Pollochaig, with his hunting knife, in 1743.

It was a particularly savage brute, one which had actually killed two children who, with their mother, were making their way across the hills. The distracted woman escaped and eventually reached Moy Hall, where she told "The Mackintosh" the terrible fate of her little ones. He at once summoned his neighbours and vassals to meet him at a certain place and hour, in order to go out and kill the brute. But MacQueen of Pollochaig was an hour late for the appointment, and The Mackintosh rebuked him with the words, "I am not used to wait for any man when such hunting as today's is afoot. Did my messenger not acquaint you with the errand we go on — the game we go after — this villainous wolf that has killed this poor widow's two bairns?"

"Oh aye, the wolf, is it?" said MacQueen casually. "The wolf to be sure. I had forgot it by now — but maybe" — and he fumbled in his plaid — "you will not be needing to go after him at all now!"

And he produced to the party assembled the gory head of a monstrous wolf; and then said he:

"As I came through the Schlock, by east the hill there, I forgaithered wi' the beast. My long dog there turned him, I buckled wi' him an' dirkit him, and syne whittled his craig, and brocht awa' his countenance for fear he micht come alive again, for they are very precarious creatures!"

"My noble Pollochaig!" cried the chief delightedly. "The deed was worthy of thee! In memorial of thy hardihood I now bestow upon thee Sennachan to yield meal for your good greyhound in all time coming!"

Some way beyond Tomatin is the Pass of Pollochaig, a wild bit of river scenery that is also called "The Streens," where for four miles the Findhorn roars and foams between steep rocks. In front of the Pass is the Hill of Treasure. It was once an island in the Findhorn Valley, and in it the Mackintoshes buried treasure belonging to them, and it was guarded from their enemies, the Cummings, by the watchful eyes of the MacQueens. Opposite the Hill of Treasure is the Hill of Parting where, local tradition has it, Ewan Cameron said good-bye to the Earl of Mar, whom he conveyed over the Monadh Liath Mountains after his defeat at Inverlochy.

A stone on top of the hill is called the Earl of Mar's Chair. In it, tradition tells, the Earl sat to eat the simple repast which was all that Cameron could procure for him, consisting of barley meal from the mill below, washed down with water from the river and drunk from the Earl's own shoe!

The old house of Pollochaig (which means the "Pool of the Little Black One"), on the southern bank of the Findhorn, was the home of the MacQueens for many hundreds of years.

Perhaps you have heard the old saying that misfortune always overtakes those who give away gifts bestowed on them by the fairies? It is strange how frequently old sayings prove their truth, and certain it is that loyalty to his friends brought misfortune to John MacQueen — "Black John of Pollochaig" — when he parted with the candles that had been a present to him from the fairies of Strathdearn.

The story is told in more than one form. Some folk insist that Black John parted with his fairy candles in order to rescue the wife of his friend, Mackintosh of Daviot; but a popular form of the story says that it was to save the wife of a humble Macgillivray clansman from the fairy hillock, that he gave them up. Whichever is the true form, the main fact is that John MacQueen of Pollochaig paid for his loyalty to his friends by offending the fairies, and that MacQueen fortunes were ever afterwards on the down-grade.

Here is the tale:

Many years ago there lived at Dumnaglass, in Inverness-shire, a Macgillivray laird named Captain Ban — which means the White Captain. He was the trusted friend of all his clansmen, one of whom came to him one day in great trouble.

"Well, Ian MacAngus Macgillivray," said Captain Ban to him, "tell me what is troubling you at all."

"Oh, Captain Ban!" the poor man said, "my wife has been stolen away by the fairies, the mischiefs! They came and told a maid who was at the milking that they have her mistress in the little hill called 'Tomshangen' or 'The Hill of the Ants.' And they said to her, 'You can tell your master that his wife will never come back to him!' I have been to the hillock over and over again, and I have heard music and dancing inside; and it is sure I am that I heard my wife's voice. She did not sound unhappy, but oh! Captain Ban, what am I to do, for the light of my life has gone out?"

"Well, that is bad enough, Ian MacAngus," said Captain Ban, "but do not be too downcast, for I think I can help you. You have heard of Black John MacQueen — the Laird of Pollochaig — of course? Well, now, he is very far in with the fairies! They even gave him a set of magic wax candles to light him into the places where they hold their merrymakings, and, if we could get one of those candles, I'm sure we could make our way into Tomshangen and rescue your wife. So listen! When to-morrow comes I will send a messenger to Black John and ask him for one of the fairy candles; and just keep your heart up until then, Ian MacAngus."

The very next morning a messenger rode off from Dunmaglass, round by the big hills: past Farr, past Moy Hall, to Pollochaig House; and there MacQueen willingly handed over one of his magic candles for Captain Ban.

"But listen now," Black John said to the man, "I'm warning you, you will not easily deliver this candle to the Captain, for the fairies will try to steal it from you. And this you must remember, that no matter what sounds you may hear behind you, you are never to look back."

When the messenger left Pollochaig it was beginning to get dark, and he had not gone very far when he heard horse's hoofs go "Klip, klop; klip, klop," behind him.

"Oho!" he said to himself, "so I am going to have company on my ride!" And he was on the point of turning round to bid the rider "Good evening" when he remembered his instructions, and rode on.

Then came the sound of carriage wheels, accompanied by strange wild music and cries of "Catch him! Catch him! Catch him!" And just as he was passing Moy Hall a weird laugh sounded so close to him that he could not help giving one little peep behind him! He saw nothing, and instantly the noises ceased. He was quite relieved — until he realised that the magic candle was no longer in his hand — and he knew the fairies had got it!

"Och, och!" he said to himself. "My grief! that I must go back and tell Captain Ban that the Little People have stolen the magic candle on me!"

A second messenger was sent to Pollochaig, and to him Black John, the Laird, gave a second fairy candle and the same instructions. This messenger was luckier than the first, for he managed to reach Farr without any misadventure. But there he heard wild weird noises behind him, which terrified him. And when loud screeches of unearthly laughter sounded "Ha, ha!" at one ear and "Hee, hee!" at the other, he could stand no more, and he whirled round upon his tormentors in desperation. But — where *were* his tormentors? He could only see behind him the big hills, looking like great black sentinels; and he could only hear the Nairn River rippling over its stony bed below. But alas! he discovered the fairy candle was gone!

"Oh! My grief!" then said the second messenger. "It is ashamed I will be to tell the White Captain this that has come upon me!"

So yet a third messenger was sent to Black John, and a third candle was given to him for Captain Ban. This time, however, the Laird of Pollochaig advised the messenger to try a different road back.

"Listen you," he said. "If you can manage to cross the Findhorn, you may beat the fairies yet, for they do not like that river. And you can go through the big hills instead of trying to go round them as the other messengers did. But remember, you *must not* look behind you!"

So the third messenger took the road to a ford on the Findhorn River, which flows through Pollochaig grounds, but when he reached the ford the river was in spate and was far too deep to cross even at the ford. So, walking backwards, he returned to Pollochaig and told the Laird his difficulty. The Laird handed a large black stone to him. "Take this," he said, "and try to span the flood with one throw of it. If you can manage that, you will be surprised at the result."

And certainly the messenger *was* surprised, for when, with a great effort, he threw the stone so that it just landed on the far bank of the flooded river, lo and behold, he found that he also was on the far bank! And now he could hear angry cries from the fairies on the other side; but they did not try to follow him, so he made his way safely through the hills and delivered the third fairy candle to Captain Ban.

Next day, Ian MacAngus Macgillivray and Captain Ban, who carried the magic candle, made their way to Tomshangen, the Ants' Hill. And whenever they lit the candle they saw a little door in the hillock, from behind which came sounds of revelry and dancing. Opening the door without knocking, they strode into the hill and there was Ian MacAngus's wife merrily dancing a reel among the fairies! When she saw her husband she stopped her dancing and said to him rather crossly;

"Oh, MacIan Angus, is that you already? Why have you come so early for me?"

"*So early!*" the affronted husband said. "Do you know it is a year and a day since you came in here?"

"Well!, well! do you tell me that?" said his wife in amazement. "I thought it was last night I came in!"

The fairies, wild with rage at the intrusion of the mortals, rushed at the two men in a threatening manner, and buzzed round them like angry bees. But the magic candle acted as a barrier, and when Ian MacAngus had got his wife outside the hillock, Captain Ban darted out after them.

"*Bang!*" went the fairy door on them, and never again did mortal eyes see the inside of Tomshangen, the Ants' Hill. But long after the good Captain Ban was dead, the magic candle was kept at Dunmaglass, and generation after generation of Macgillivrays were told how their ancestor, the White Captain, had got the better of the fairy folk of Strathdearn.

The Prince and Princess of Isle Maree

One of the loveliest of Scottish lochs lies in the heart of Ross-shire and is called Loch Maree, after a saintly old man named "Maelrubha" (pronounced "Marooee") who lived on one of its islands.

That was many centuries ago, in days when a powerful race from across the North Sea used to invade our coasts. They came in great dragon-shaped boats and seized the beautiful fertile lands of the West, and they killed, or drove away, the rightful owners, who were not powerful enough to oppose the big yellow-haired Norsemen.

Now here is the love story of one of these Norsemen, who in his own country was a great Prince.

He had sailed his galleys into a sea loch which is connected with Loch Maree by the River Ewe, and there his fleet lay.

It was a splendid harbour from which to raid other parts of the coast, and the forests around provided fine hunting for him and his followers, and he looked upon the whole district as his own.

One day, when hunting in the forest, he spied a very beautiful girl, with whom he fell head over heels in love. "Who can she be — this maiden — whose eyes are like the stars, her skin like the lily, her cheeks like the rose, and her hair like the raven's wing?" he cried. "Find out where she lives. I must have her for my wife!"

So his people went all through the west of Ross inquiring about her. Before long they were able to tell him that she was of ancient descent, and that her father and his forbears had been owners of Loch Maree and all the country round it until driven

out by the Norsemen. Immediately the Prince went to the old Chief and told him that he wished to marry his daughter, only to be met with a proud refusal.

"You have seized my home, my lands, and my cattle," the old man said. "I was not strong enough to stand out against you — but I can and will prevent you from taking away my daughter." Then to the amazement of all, his daughter, blushing hotly, stepped forward and said:

"But, father, have *I* no say in the matter? What if I wish to marry this young man?"

"Marry a stranger!" the old man exclaimed in amazement. "Surely, my daughter, that is impossible! Why, you have never seen him before!"

"Oh, father," she murmured, "often and often I have watched him sailing his great galley which lies in Poolewe, or hunting in our woods by Loch Maree; and I have never seen anyone to compare with him for strength or beauty!"

At these words the Prince gave a great cry of joy and swept her into his arms.

"Come!" he cried, "come with me to the holy man of Loch Maree, and let him marry us!"

And to the old Chief he said:

"The lands which were yours are yours till death. We will govern them together!"

Then followed many months of perfect happiness for the yellow-haired Prince and his beautiful bride.

But a life of ease and inaction did not content the other Norsemen. They missed the excitement and adventure to which they were accustomed, and by and by they threatened to leave the Prince and return across the seas unless he agreed to lead them again on a raiding expedition.

The Prince could not bear to lose his splendid fleet, so he had to break the news to his wife that, for a time, he must leave her, and go sailing with his galleys. Inconsolable at the thought of parting from her husband the pretty Princess cried:

"How can I live without you now? and *where* can I live? My

maidens and I will not be safe without you, and my father is now very old and infirm."

"As to that," the Prince replied, "I have spoken to the holy man, Maelrubha, and he has offered to be your guardian while I am away.

"You and your maidens will be perfectly safe in his care; you will live in a stronghold which we shall build beside his chapel on Isle Maree, and there you will stay until I can return to claim my treasure. And oh, my beloved," he cried, "you know that every minute I am away from you will seem like an hour, every hour like a day, and every day like a year!

"But the time will pass — then love will fill the sails of my galley and carry me swiftly back to you!"

They made elaborate plans for meeting again:

"When my galley sails up the River Ewe," the Prince said, "if all is well I shall hoist a blue flag at the foremast."

"And when I see your galley," said the Princess, "I shall embark with my maidens on my barge to meet you; and I also will hoist a blue flag, as a signal that my love has been true to you."

"But should anything be wrong with either of us, let a black flag at the mast be our signal," he said, "though indeed, my love, I could never survive if I were to lose you now!"

So they parted, and when a year had passed the Princess watched anxiously for the return of his galley.

"Oh, why does he not come?" she wept to her maidens. "The days go so slowly! What can he be doing all this long time?"

Now one of her maidens, who had long been jealous of the Princess, took this opportunity to drop a little seed of distrust into her heart.

"What if he has reached his own land and found a golden-haired lady to console him for your absence?" she said to the Princess, adding:

"I have been told that the Norse maidens are beautiful as the rising sun!"

"But surely the contrast between the Prince, with his golden hair, and our Princess with hair like night or the raven's wing was one of the things that attracted them to each other," said another.

"You can never tell," said the mischief maker. "After all, 'like draws to like' they say!"

So the seed of distrust took root in the heart of the Princess and grew as the days passed; but she never confided her trouble to the holy man, and when he saw how she got paler, day by day, he thought she was lonely, and said:

"Do not look so mournful, my daughter. He will return soon."

At last one day, a galley was seen making its way up the River Ewe, with outspread sails and a blue flag at its foremast.

Then, with her heart throbbing with jealous pangs, the Princess resolved on a desperate plan.

"Come," she said to her maidens, "let me test his love!"

So she made a sort of couch, all covered with white, on the deck of her barge, and on it, clothed in a gown of white, she lay with eyes closed.

"Oh," cried some of her maidens, "it is not lucky to do this! You look like a dead bride, and to see you like this would break the Prince's heart!"

But the jealous maiden said:

"Say, rather, that our mistress looks like a dead white bird, slain by a shaft from a mortal!"

This fired the imagination of the Princess, for she said:

"I shall stay as I am. Group yourselves round me like mourners, and hoist the black flag at the foremast; and then let us meet the Prince's galley. When he comes I shall know by his bearing whether he still loves me!"

Meanwhile the Prince was gazing from his galley, anxiously watching for the first glimpse of the barge of his beloved. Soon he saw what looked like a moving speck far away among the islands of Loch Maree, and as the two vessels drew nearer he realized with horror that the the flag at the mast of the barge was not dark blue, as he at first imagined, but *black!*

"What can have happened to my beloved one?" he cried, urging the rowers to speed up.

Nearer came the two vessels; then alongside each other — and the Prince leapt on the deck of the barge.

There lay his wife, white and still, and round her — their heads sunk as if in silent grief — were grouped her maidens.

"What? Dead?" he cried. "My beautiful bride! Then indeed I will live no longer!" And before a hand could be lifted to stay him he had seized his dagger and plunged it into his heart!

Up sprang the Princess with a terrible cry when she saw this proof of her husband's grief — but it was too late!

So in an agony of remorse she seized the fatal dagger and plunged it into her own heart!

They laid the lovers to rest on Isle Maree, where two roughly sculptured stone crosses marked their graves.

In the stillness of a summer's evening, old folks say they can hear the splash of oars, and strange cries of despair — weird echoes of those tragic happenings of long ago.

But from the leafy branches of the trees that wave over the two graves comes the tender cooing of a pair of turtle-doves!

Eoghan MacGabhar, the Son of the Goat

Part 1 — How Eoghan and Flora came to Ardlair

I don't suppose you have ever heard of Eoghan MacGabhar, which means Son of the Goat? It is an old wife's tale — but it rings true.

Over six hundred years ago there lived at Ardlair, near the west end of Loch Maree, an old woman named Oighrig, with her son Kenneth. Theirs was a simple life. Most of their food was raised on their own little bit of ground, and the milk with which they washed it down came from their pet goat, Earba, who usually gave them an abundant supply. But one spring, Earba puzzled her owners by giving very little milk, and they began to think that someone else must be milking her. So said Oighrig to her son:

"Kenneth, lad, to-morrow you will follow Earba, and see, if you can, who is stealing her milk. If the thieves are human, we must do something to stop them. But if it is the fairies, Kenneth, that is a bad job indeed, for we can do nothing to *them*, at all, at all!"

Early next morning Kenneth set out after Earba, and lucky it was for him that he was nimble of foot! For Earba made straight for a dark cave high up on the face of a steep rock. And as Kenneth carefully picked his steps up the rock he saw, to his amazement, a little boy dart out of the cave and begin to fondle the goat.

His first thought was, "Now isn't my mother the wise woman, for indeed that is a fairy boy, and sure he has bewitched Earba!" But when a beautiful girl came out of the cave and sat down to milk the goat, Kenneth said to himself, "No, it is not

fairies at all, for indeed no fairy was ever so beautiful as that!"

Reaching the rocky ledge he leapt up and faced the startled milker.

"Fear not, lady," he said, "I am not here to harm you — indeed, who would expect to find a living being in such a place? I was only wanting to see where our goat, Earba — truant that she is! — has been spending her time."

"Well, and glad enough we were to find such a place," said the girl, "for it is hiding we are, and but for your kindly goat we would have starved." Then — hesitating — she said:

"I cannot tell you all our story, but my name is Flora, and this is Eoghan MacGabhar. Together we have fled for our lives!"

"Tell me no more, lady, but follow me," said Kenneth. "I can show you an easy way down the cliff, and you shall come to our cottage, where my mother will be kind to you."

And when the young fugitives were welcomed, as though they belonged to that humble home, they could scarcely believe in their good fortune.

They had brought two treasures with them from the cave. One was a beautiful robe of state, made of scarlet velvet, bound and fringed with pure gold. The other was a sword on whose hilt of ivory and gold strange characters were engraved.

With true Highland courtesy mother and son asked no questions of their visitors, although — as was natural — they often wondered who they might be. And Oighrig, seeing how Kenneth's eyes followed Flora everywhere, said:

"Kenneth, lad, we must not forget that these guests of ours are not like us. Indeed, it is sure I am that they are of *kingly* blood."

But Oighrig's caution came too late, for Kenneth was already deeply in love with Flora.

One day it chanced that the great Lord of Kintail from the Castle of Eilean Donan came hunting along Maree side; and seeing Flora and the boy at the cottage door, he said to

Oighrig:

"Tell me, mother, who are your visitors?"

Before Oighrig could answer, Kenneth answered hastily:

"That is Flora, my wife, and the boy is her kinsman. He is called Eoghan MacGabhar, the Son of the Goat."

At that name the Lord of Kintail started, for he remembered an old clan saying that with the son of a goat ill-fortune would come to Kintail. But he heeded it not, for he was bewitched with Flora's beauty. And he answered Kenneth scornfully:

"She is no wife of yours! Have I not eyes to see that she is far above you?"

So poor Kenneth's story had served no purpose!

Flora eyed the newcomer coldly, for she liked not his bold looks, but again and again he returned to Ardlair to see her. And one day he told the unhappy girl that unless she would go with him to his Castle of Eilean Donan he would have Oighrig and Kenneth turned out of their little home and their bit of ground laid waste.

That night Flora tossed, sleepless, in her bed.

"Oh!" she thought, miserably, "how can I bring misfortune on those who have been so kind to me? No! Sooner than that I shall go away; and, even if I perish among the mountains, I shall at least save my friends. I know they will be good to Eoghan."

And with the thought she rose quietly and stole softly to the door.

But that night Kenneth slept lightly, and, hearing a gentle movement at the door, he rose from his couch of bracken just in time to keep Flora from stealing out into the dark night.

The unusual sounds drew Oighrig also from her bed, and she took the now weeping Flora in her arms and tried to comfort her. When Flora had told her tale and begged to be allowed to go away, Kenneth said:

"Flora, I love you! Yes, even although I know that you are far above me! So let me serve you now by going with you. My mother and Eoghan will come too. What say you?"

Then Flora, holding out her hands to him, said simply:

"Kenneth! You see it is because I love you that I feel I ought to leave you!"

Then indeed Oighrig's heart was glad for her son!

They all agreed that it would be best to leave the place, so next night saw the little household, under cover of darkness, stealing towards Poolewe with the faithful goat in attendance. They carried with them, of course, the velvet robe and the sword of state.

But they were not to escape the Lord of Kintail; for, all unknown to them, their movements had been carefully watched. When they reached Poolewe they saw a vessel lying, and a boat was being rowed ashore from her.

Hand in hand Kenneth and Flora went down to meet the boat, meaning to ask for a passage to the islands, or anywhere out of reach of the Lord of Kintail. But what was their dismay, when the boat came close, to see from the tartan of the rowers that they were Eilean Donan men! Kenneth and Flora fled like deer, but the ground was rough for Flora and they were overtaken and carried off, leaving Oighrig and Eoghan horror-stricken on the shore.

When the vessel reached Eilean Donan, Kenneth and Flora were separated. He was put among the Castle retainers; and Flora was taken to the Lord of the Castle, who said to her triumphantly:

"See you, Flora, jewel of my heart, was I not telling you that you would be here? Now, look at me and tell me, is it possible to compare that herd fellow, that clod, with me?"

But Flora stood with eyes turned away from him.

"Well," said the Lord of Kintail, "if you will not look at me, look around you, and see what I have to offer you. This great Castle, firm on its proud rock! Loch Duich — as lovely in its way as Loch Maree — and the beautiful country that lies around it! The mountains of Kintail that they call the Five Sisters! All is mine, and all may be yours if you will but marry me."

At that Flora raised her head proudly and, looking him in

the eyes, she said:

"My Lord of Kintail and Eilean Donan, you may own the length and breadth of Scotland for all I care! But *me* you will never own, for I belong to Kenneth!"

The great lord was persuasive, passionate, tender — but nothing would move Flora, and "It is Kenneth I love!" was her only reply to his pleading.

His wooing, however, was rudely interrupted when news came to Eilean Donan that the Earl of Ross was raiding Kinlochewe, and Kintail bristled with warlike preparations!

Now was Kenneth's chance to make good, and in the fierce fighting against the men of Ross his claymore flashed like lightning, dealing destruction with every flash. And many was the stout blow he struck for Kintail, for he was indeed a born fighter. After the campaign was over the Lord of Kintail (whose love had had time to cool) showed his gratitude to Kenneth by letting him marry Flora, and by giving him an important post in his service. And only the uncertainty of what had happened to Oighrig and Eoghan kept Kenneth and Flora from being the very happiest couple in all the Highlands!

Part II — How Eoghan got back his kingdom

When Kenneth and Flora were taken captive by the men of Eilean Donan and put aboard the vessel for Kintail, Oighrig, Kenneth's mother, and Eoghan, Flora's young charge, were left on the beach at Poolewe. Their only possessions were the sword of state and the velvet mantle that had been brought from the cave where Kenneth found them, and, of course, the faithful goat, Earba.

While they were wondering what they should do, a vessel came into the bay, and they begged the Captain to take them aboard and let them go after Flora and Kenneth to Eilean Donan. The Captain agreed, and in high hopes they set sail. But, as it turned out, he had no intention of going to Kintail, and

he landed the old woman and the boy and Earba in the country
of a great Chief named Mic Ailean Mor. When they landed, the
Chief happened to be hunting near the shore, and he went
down to see who the new arrivals might be. Having questioned
them and having seen the mantle and the sword, he guessed
that Eoghan must be of noble descent. So he took him to his
Castle and brought him up with his own sons as a warrior and a
gentleman.

He was very kind to Oighrig too. He gave her a cosy little
hut beside the Castle, and a cow for her own use, besides
providing for the goat, Earba. And Eoghan continually went to
see the good old woman there.

He grew up to be a strong, brave youth whom no one could
match as a fighter. When Eoghan was eighteen, orders came
from the King of Scotland that war was to be made against a
great island kingdom, whose ruler was the queen-widow of a
famous Norse King named Olaf Mor.

The royal summons was sent to Kintail also, and the great
lord there combined his forces with those of Mic Ailean Mor —
amounting to 20,000 men between them.   Eoghan, all
eagerness to fight, was put in charge of a thousand men. While
they were getting ready a slim Highlander offered his services
as Eoghan's page. But Eoghan looked at him with a smile,
saying, "What use could you be to me in battle?" You are not tall
enough and you are, besides, so slender, almost like a woman"
— and the page flushed scarlet. But every day he was there and
soon he proved so handy that Eoghan said at last, with a laugh,
"Well, if you are determined on coming with me, you can look
after the baggage, and save a man." And the page seemed
content with anything, so that he might follow Eoghan.

Soon they went into action, and at first all went well with the
forces of Kintail and Mic Ailean Mor. They got possession of the
island of Mull, which they plundered and burnt. They then put
to sea in their vast fleet of vessels, which they anchored in a sea
loch.

Some of the troops went on shore to invade and plunder

the mainland, but the chiefs and their principal followers stayed for the night on board the vessels. But when morning broke, lo and behold! they found that the Queen's fleet had come into the loch in the darkness of night and had completely surrounded them.

Mic Ailean Mor, with two sons and Eoghan MacGabhar, were taken captive. So also was the Lord of Kintail, with many of his relations and followers, and they were all marched before the gallant — but apparently merciless — Queen, who in a passionate speech said:

"Look you, slaves! — for you *are* slaves! — of a tyrant who persecutes, and thinks to destroy the royal race to which I belong! Look to yourselves, I say! For now vengeance is mine, and this is my decree!"

And she went on to order that next morning at 9 o'clock all the prisoners were to be brought out, seven by seven, beginning with the youngest, and hanged before her eyes!

At this terrible sentence a tense silence was broken by a sudden scream. It came from the page of Eoghan MacGabhar. And the Queen, gazing with scorn at his pale face and shaking hands, cried: "Oh, coward heart! Do they call *you* a man?"

Morning came, and seven youths, the youngest of the warriors, were led out to the place of execution. At their head, and bearing himself as proudly as if he was going to his coronation instead of his execution, was Eoghan MacGabhar; and he wore the scarlet velvet mantle fringed with gold, and carried the richly ornamented sword with which his page had insisted on investing him.

The Queen's eye was caught by the scarlet gleam. She looked — and looked again, started and half rose, and then, screaming "Mac Olaf Mor! Mac Olaf Mor!" (which means "Son of Olaf the Great") she fell to the ground in a dead faint.

But what was this! Without a glance at the fallen Queen, her chiefs and kinsmen were rushing forward, and kneeling down round Eoghan MacGabhar!

For they too had recognized him, and he was none other

than the son of the Queen and Olaf the Great! They raised him on their shoulders and set him on the very throne from which his mother had condemned him to die!

When the Queen recovered she demanded to know how this wonderful thing had come about, and how her son, who had disappeared in his childhood, came there. The page now came forward, and kneeling at the Queen's feet she pulled off her cap — when down fell a mass of golden hair. It was *Flora,* the Queen's young sister, who, faithful to her charge, and unknown to Kenneth, had followed Eoghan MacGabhar into battle.

"Listen," she said to her deeply interested audience, "when Eoghan's father died, a dark plot was made to kill the boy. You, sister, were so overcome with grief at the death of Olaf Mor that I spared you hearing it. But, day and night, I never left Eoghan.

"One night the wife of one of the plotters (to whose child I had been kind) came and told me that if I would save the boy's life I should take him away at once. So, leaving a message for you, sister, we fled that night."

"That message," said the Queen, "I never received. I thought that you and my son had been murdered, and I lived but for vengeance!"

Then Flora told of their flight, and of its end in the cave at Ardlair; of how the goat, Earba, led Kenneth to them, of the kindness they had received in that humble cottage — and of all the adventures which followed.

The Queen joyfully gave up her place to her son, whose first act as King was to release all those who had been condemned to die.

A firm alliance was formed between the Clans of Kintail and Mic Ailean Mor on the one side and the descendants of Olaf the Great on the other. Kenneth and Flora went to live at Eoghan's Castle, where, as long as she lived, Oighrig also was an honoured guest. And it is said that the descendants of Earba, the goat, are to be seen in the West to this day! Eoghan married a daughter of the house of Kintail, and helped by his friendship to increase the power and standing of that great clan.

In the West they still have the old saying, which came true in those days of long ago:

> "The Son of the Goat shall triumphantly bear
> The mountain on flame and the horns of the deer.
> From Forest of Loyne to the hill of Ben Croshen
> From mountain to vale and from ocean to ocean."

The grey horse and the widow's daughters

There was once a poor widow who lived in the Highlands with her three daughters. They were all fair to look upon, and indeed the young men admired them; but they had no tocher, so there was no word of them getting married.

All the widow had besides her cottage was a yard full of fine kail, which was the principal food of the household. But there was a big grey horse that would come, morning after morning, and feed upon the kail, and, try as they liked, he would not be driven away.

One day the eldest of the three daughters said:

"Well indeed, mother, we must do *something* to keep the beast from eating all the kail on us! See you — to-morrow morning I'll take my spinning wheel and go and sit in the yard, and when he comes I'll try if I cannot drive him away."

"That's you for a brave lassie," said the widow. "When he comes in, just you give him the good hit with your distaff, and maybe he will not be coming again."

So the next morning when the horse arrived as usual, there was the eldest daughter spinning among the kail. Up she got in a fine rage, and, taking her distaff, over she went to him and gave him one crack! But, och! och! — when she did, it was herself got the fine fright, for the distaff stuck to the horse, and her hand stuck in the distaff; and away went the horse — gallop, gallop — and she with him, to a green hillock not far away.

And there the horse stamped three times on the hillock, and called out:

"Open, open, green hillock, and let in the grey horse that is son of a King! Open, open, green hillock, and let in the widow's eldest daughter!"

And the hillock opened — but it wasn't the inside of a hill they were in at all, but a beautiful Palace! And the eldest daughter found warm water waiting to wash her feet, and a soft bed to lie upon, and beautiful clothes to wear.

In the morning the grey horse came to her and said:

"Well now, I am going to the hunting today. See you and prepare a good dinner for me. Here are the keys of this Palace. You can open the door of every room that is in it — all but the one that this little key is for. Swear to me that you will not open it."

So she promised she would leave that room alone, and the grey horse said, "Remember, if you are a good girl while I am away I will marry you before very long," and off he cantered.

The girl went into the grandest kitchen she had ever seen, and made ready a fine dinner; and then she thought she would see what the Palace was like; so she opened room after room, and each seemed more magnificent than the last.

Then, of course, she began to think about the forbidden room.

"I wonder what can be in it! If I give just one peep, who will be the wiser, and where will be the harm?" she thought. So she turned the key and opened the door a little way. But what she saw put the fear on her so that she fell into the room on her hands and knees; and when she was able to rise, her hands were all over blood! For the room was full of poor dead ladies — a fearsome sight indeed!

She tried to wash the blood off her hands, but she could not get the stains out.

"Oh dear, oh dear!" she sobbed in teror, "what am I to do?"

Then there came a small lean cat to her feet, and it said:

"Give me a plate of milk — even a little drop — and I will lick the hands of you until they are clean."

But she said:

"And if good warm water will not take out the stains, is it

likely that a cat's tongue will? Shoo! Off you go! Ugly little beast!"

As she spoke, home came the grey horse himself, all pleased with his hunting, and asked for his food. As he ate he said:

"Well. wast thou a good little woman to-day?"

"Oh yes, I think so," was her reply.

"Let me see thy hands and I will know whether thou speakest the truth," he said, as he opened her clenched hands. And there was the blood on them!

"Oho!" he said to the terrified girl. "So that is the way of it!" And he took an axe and chopped her head clean off, and he threw her into the forbidden room — and went on with his meal.

Next morning the grey horse was feeding once more on the widow's kail; and the second daughter said to her mother:

"Well, mother, *I* am going out this morning to see if I cannot drive that beast from among our precious kail."

And the widow said:

"That's you for a brave lassie!"

So out the second daughter went, taking with her a seam she was sewing, and she went right up to the horse and stabbed him with her needle. But could she get it away again? No — nor the hand that held the needle! And away the horse went, and the girl with him, to the green hillock.

He stamped his hoofs and called out as before:

"Open, open, green hillock, and let in the grey horse that is son of a King! Open, open, green hillock, and let in the widow's second daughter!"

And the hillock opened, and in they went; and everything happened as it had done before.

Next morning the grey horse gave the widow's second daughter the keys of the Palace, warning her by all she ever saw not to use the key of the closed chamber. And, telling her to have ie dinner ready for him when he returned from the huntine went away and left her preparing the dinner.

ƒ she finished doing that, she began opening up the room the Palace and admiring all the beautiful things in them.1d after looking again and again at the key of the forbid room, she could no longer resist the temptation to peep it, and she gently opened the door.

Ehat she saw made her let out a scream, for there was her si.lying among a lot of poor dead ladies! And the fright made fall on her hands and knees in the room, and when she rap one of her hands was all over blood. She ran for warmer and scrubbed it again and again, without being able tt it cleaned — and terror came upon her.

T came the little lean cat, saying as before:

"ll lick thy hand as clean as ever for a plate of milk."

Ell the answer it got from her was:

"ᵗ little beast, be going with you! If the good warm water ɪot cleanse my hand, is it likely that your tongue can? Shoo!

" then, you will see what will happen when himself comeme!" said the cat, and it sat down and began licking itself.

T came the sound of the horse's gallop, and he came in anded for his dinner. And when it was set before him he said te second daughter:

", wast thou a good little woman to-day?"

"ᵗ I was," said she, shivering all the same.

"ne see thy hands," he said, "and I will know."

Spread her clean hand over the stained one, but he pulled the other hand from below, and when he saw the stainsho!" he said, "so that is the way of it!"

Ae took his axe and chopped off her head, and then he threw into the chamber beside her sister.

ƒnext morning the youngest sister, who was knitting besidr mother, saw the grey horse back again among the kail. Both her sisters had disappeared, and neither she nor her mother had closed an eye all night, wondering what had happened to them. But she said to her mother in a brave voice:

"Well, mother, I am going out to see whether I cannot find out where my sisters have gone, and if necessary I, too, will go with the grey horse and look for them."

"You're a brave lassie," said the widow, "but mind you come back to me."

So out went the youngest daughter, and over to the grey horse.

"Where are my sisters?" she said, and she stuck her knitting needle in his side. It stuck to him and her hand stuck to the knitting needle, and off they went to the green hillock. Again he stamped his hoofs and called out:

"Open, open, green hillock, and let in the grey horse that is son of a King! Open, open, green hillock, and let in the widow's youngest daughter!"

And everything happened to her as it had to her sisters, whom she saw next day, dead, in the forbidden chamber. With the shock of it she fell down, and her hands also became stained with blood; and although she tried and tried to wash them, the stains would not disappear.

But when the little cat came to her with its offer to lick her hands clean in return for a drop of milk, she did not repulse it as her sisters had done. Her answer was:

"Look you — creature that you are — if you will do what you are promising and lick my hands clean, you are worth a good drink of milk. So come and take it."

And after the cat had lapped its fill of milk, it licked and licked the girl's hands until there was not a stain upon them.

So when the grey horse galloped home in the gloaming to get his dinner there was no fear in her heart. And when he asked to look at her hands and saw not one spot on them he was very pleased indeed with her, and he said:

"Aha! thou art not like thy sisters; and if thou wilt be good for a few more days, thyself and myself will be married."

And he went away again the next day to the hunting.

Then the little cat came and sat beside the girl, and it said:

"See now, if you have a wish to marry a King's son I will tell you how to accomplish it. In the treasure-room of this Palace there are a number of old chests. Take out three of them and clean them up and then say to the grey horse that they can easily be spared, and that you would like him to leave them, one at a time, at your mother's house. And tell him that he must on no account look inside them, for you will be spying from the tree-tops and will call out to him if he does. Now, if you look above the door of the treasure-room you will find a magic sword, which you must take down when the grey horse has gone hunting to-morrow. Take it into the forbidden room and wave it over your sisters, and they will come alive again. Then put them each into one of the chests, along with some of the jewels from the treasure-room, close the lids, and get the grey horse to carry the chests, one at a time, to your mother. When he has done what you ask, instruct him to carry the third chest also, and, taking with you the magic sword, slip into the chest when he is not looking, and he will carry you home. After this third journey the horse will return to the Palace, and when he finds that you are not there he will go back to your mother's cottage. You must be waiting there for him, and when you have a chance you must lay the magic sword hard to his neck, and you will then see how you are going to find the King's son."

The third daughter thanked the little cat and did exactly as it bade her. She restored her sisters to life by waving the magic sword over them; she put them in two of the chests and heaped in gold and jewels from the treasure-room along with them; and she told them what to say if the horse tried to see what he was carrying. She found him quite willing to do as she asked — though he certainly wondered what she had put in the chests; and when he came to a spot in the glen where he thought he would not be seen he tried to peep in. Immediately a voice came from — he knew not where — and it said:

"Who is peeping? Who is peeping?"

And thinking that the sound came from the tree-tops he laughed and said, "Well, well! Surely thou hast the good sight!" — and went on with his burden. And when the third chest also was delivered at the widow's cottage, the horse went home for his dinner.

When he found no dinner and no one waiting to welcome him, he galloped back to the widow's cottage in a great state. The door was closed, but he crashed it through with his forehead. Behind the door the youngest daughter was waiting with the magic sword in her hand, and when his head crashed through, she brought the sword down on his neck with all her might, and he changed immediately into a beautiful youth!

"Oh!" she cried in wonder. "It is true, then — you are the King's son!"

"I am that, indeed," he replied, "and more than that, I am your husband-to-be."

And he took her hand, and leading her to the widow, he said:

"Mother, this third daughter of yours has broken an evil spell that bound me. Will you give her to me, for indeed I love her truly?"

And the widow gave a glad consent.

Thanks to this same girl she had got back her two elder daughters, and with them enough gold and jewels to ensure good husbands for them and comfort for herself for the rest of her life.

When the King's son took his bride home to his Palace, they found a pretty girl there who ran to the Prince and kissed him affectionately.

"Why, who is this?" said the young bride in astonishment.

"Who but my sister," he answered — "my sister, who was the little lean cat! At the same time as you released me you released her from the spell that had changed her. She will be a sister to you and will live with us until she marries," — and the two girls embraced each other tenderly.

They lived happily in the Palace under the hill, and many a time did the widow bless the day that brought the grey horse to eat her kail!